# America's Game

# Texas Rangers

## Bob Italia

ABDO & Daughters
PUBLISHING

Published by Abdo & Daughters, 4940 Viking Dr., Suite 622, Edina, MN 55435.

Cover photo: Allsport
Interior photos: Allsport, pages 1, 5.
Wide World Photo, pages 6, 9, 10, 13, 14, 16, 17, 21-28.

Edited by Paul Joseph

**Library of Congress Cataloging–in–Publication Data**

Italia, Bob, 1955–
   Texas Rangers / Bob Italia
      p. cm. — (America's game)
   Includes index.
   Summary: Examines the history and notable players of the baseball team that began in Washington, D.C., as the Senators.
   ISBN 1-56239-678-1
   1. Texas Rangers (Baseball team)—History [1. Texas Rangers (Baseball team)—History. 2. Baseball—History.]
I. Title. II. Series.
GV875.T4I83 1997
796.357'64'09764531—dc20         96-23795
                           CIP

# Contents

# Texas Rangers

Despite the fact that the Texas Rangers have had many star players, the team is still in search of its first championship season. The Rangers began this quest in Washington, D.C., as the new Senators, who are best remembered for their slugger, Frank Howard.

The Senators played 11 futile seasons in the nation's capital, never finishing better than 15 games back. Then they moved to their present home in Arlington, Texas.

Between 1961 and 1971, the Washington Senators had four well-known managers—Mickey Vernon, Gil Hodges, Jim Lemon, and Ted Williams—but little success. They lost 100 or more games in each of their first 4 years. Their only winning season came in 1969, when they finished fourth in the American League West with an 86-76 record. The team played much better in Texas, even though they lost 100 games in 1972, their first season, and 105 the next.

In the late 1970s, the Rangers finished second in 1977 and 1978 and third in 1979. After a good showing in the 1981 strike season, the Rangers again fell on hard times. But then they revived in the late 1980s when fireballer Nolan Ryan joined the team.

In 1996, sluggers Juan Gonzalez, Dean Palmer, and Will Clark led a potent Ranger attack to its first division title. Should Texas assemble a solid pitching staff, fans may soon be cheering for their first World Series title.

Juan Gonzales in a
1994 game against the
Kansas City Royals.

Gil Hodges, former star first baseman for the New York Mets and for the Dodgers of Los Angeles and Brooklyn, buttons up a Washington uniform after being named the Senators' manager in 1963.

# The Washington Senators

The Texas Rangers began their short history in 1961 in Washington, D.C., as the Washington Senators. In the 1950s, the Senators were in last place four times. Not once in the decade did they finish first in the American League.

Owner Calvin Griffin wanted to move his Senators to Minnesota. He succeeded—but with the understanding that a new expansion team would be granted to Washington, D.C. This kept Major League Baseball in the nation's capital.

The new Washington Senators opened the 1961 season with players such as Gene Woodling, Dale Long, Willie Tasby, and Dick Donovan. Mickey Vernon was the manager. The team looked respectable, but the Senators finished in a tie with the Kansas City Athletics for last place. Donovan had the best ERA in the league, but only a 10-10 record. The Senators traded him with Gene Green, the team's home run leader, and Jim Mahoney for outfielder Jimmy Piersall, who was hitting .322 for Cleveland. But Piersall fell to .244 with Washington.

The Senators moved into their new home, D.C. Stadium—later renamed RFK Stadium—the following season. The move did not help. The team dropped to last place in 1962 and 1963. They were the worst in the American League in hitting, fielding, and pitching.

During the 1963 season, Gil Hodges replaced Vernon as manager, but the team could not escape the cellar. The 1964 Senators lost 100 games. But they edged out the Kansas City Royals for ninth place. Even better, pitchers Claude Osteen (15-13) and Ron Kline (10-7) had winning records. But after four seasons, the new Washington Senators had a combined .370 winning percentage, with no improvement in sight. And they had few stars. Outfielder Chuck Hinton batted .310 in 1962, third best in the league.

# Big Frank

The first ray of hope joined the team in a multi-player trade with the Los Angeles Dodgers in December 1964. He was outfielder Frank Howard. Howard stood 6' 7" and weighed 255 pounds. The ex-basketball and baseball player from Ohio State had been a Dodger for five seasons. In 1960, he belted 23 homers and won Rookie of the Year honors. His greatest moment came in the 1963 World Series when his fifth-inning home run off New York Yankee ace Whitey Ford—a tape-measure shot into the upper deck of left field at Dodger Stadium—put Los Angeles ahead of the Yankees in Game 4. The Dodgers went on to sweep the Yankees in four games.

Howard was not just a superstar for the Senators. He was their *only* superstar. In his first year with the Senators, he belted 21 homers. From 1969 to 1971, his home run totals read 44, 48, 44. In all, he led the Senators in homers for seven seasons in a row. He also had the highest batting average on the team for six of those seasons. In 1969, when the Ted Williams-led team made a run for the title, Howard batted .296, slammed 48 home runs, scored 111 runs, drove in another 111, and had a slugging average of .574.

At RFK Stadium, white paint marked some of the seats where Howard's homers landed. Before long, the upper deck in left field was dotted with white seats.

In 1965, the Senators moved up to eighth place. They stayed there in 1966, and then finished sixth in 1967. Except for Howard and third baseman Ken McMullen, the Senators lacked star power. Hodges left after the 1967 season. Jim Lemon, a former slugger with the original Senators, replaced Hodges. He had one 10th-place season before departing.

Washington Senators' slugger Frank Howard is ready to
connect for a ninth-inning home run in a 1968 game against
Detroit. It would be Howard's eighth homer in five games,
breaking the major league record set by Babe Ruth in 1921.

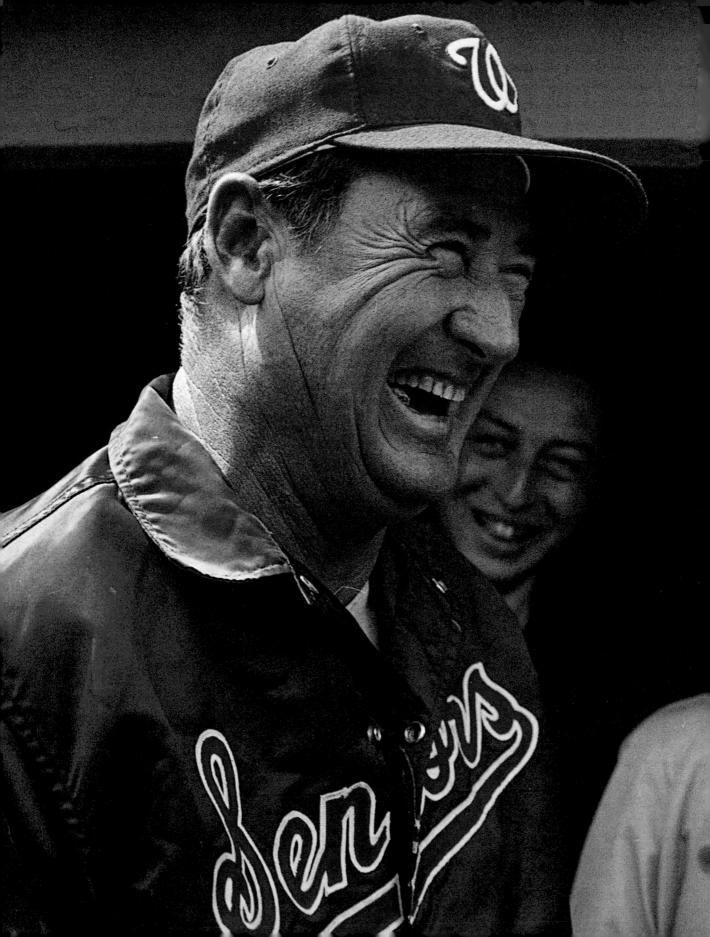

# Ted Williams

Divisional play began in 1969. That meant that sixth place became last place in both divisions of the American League. Hall-of-Famer Ted Williams signed on as manager and worked a minor miracle. The Senators finished fourth in the AL East, 23 games back. But more importantly, they won more games than they lost—finally giving fans hope for the future.

Pitcher Dick Bosman had a 14-5 record with a league-leading 2.19 ERA. Reliever Darold Knowles went 9-2 with a 2.24 ERA. Frank Howard smacked 48 home runs, and first baseman Mike Epstein launched a career-high 30 home runs. The Senators also had the second-highest turnout in 71 years of Major League Baseball in Washington.

Washington's surprising 86-76 record earned Ted Williams AL Manager of the Year honors, raising hopes for the 1970 season. But that year, the Senators fell into last place with a 70-92 record. The few bright spots were Bosman's 16-12 record, Howard's league-leading 44 home runs and 126 RBIs, and Epstein's 20 homers. Knowles also had 27 saves with a 2.04 ERA.

In 1971, the Senators improved to fifth place. But their record declined to 63-96. Epstein had been traded to the Oakland A's for Don Mincher, a veteran first baseman nearing the end of his career. Mincher hit for a higher average than Epstein but with less power.

*Facing page:* Former Red Sox slugger Ted Williams returns to Fenway Park in Boston as manager of the Senators.

# Heading South

Owner Bob Short, who had bought the Senators in December 1968, was determined to make big changes. The first was to move the team to the Dallas-Fort Worth area. On September 21, 1971, the Baseball Owners Association voted 10-2 to allow Short to take the Senators to Texas.

The new Texas Rangers would play in minor-league Arlington Stadium, which was quickly renovated to hold 35,694 fans. The first-year Rangers were 54-100, and finished $38^{1}/2$ games behind first-place Oakland. Even worse, they finished $20^{1}/2$ games behind 5th-place California. Ted Williams decided to resign. Whitey Herzog replaced him. But the Rangers had much rebuilding to do.

There were some stars on the Texas team, such as slugging outfielder Jeff Burroughs and first baseman Jim Spencer. But the Rangers had no pitching. Only young Jim Bibby, with his 9-10 record and 3.24 ERA, looked promising. The Rangers were 47-91 when Herzog was fired. Texas finished a distant last.

Billy Martin managed the Rangers in 1974.

# Billy Martin And Company

The following season, Billy Martin signed on as manager. He had worked wonders for the Minnesota Twins and Detroit Tigers, and was expected to do the same in Texas.

Martin got some pitching help by acquiring veteran Ferguson Jenkins from the Chicago Cubs. Jenkins finished with a 25-12 record and a 2.83 ERA. And Jim Bibby won 19 games. Jeff Burroughs hit .301, belted 25 homers, and drove in 118 runs on his way to the American League MVP Award. Shortstop Toby Harrah was second on the team with 21 home runs and 74 RBIs. First baseman Mike Hargrove hit .323 with 62 RBIs and was named AL Rookie of the Year. Infielder Lenny Randle batted .302 and drove in 49 runs. And veteran outfielder Cesar Tovar hit .292 and drove in 59 runs. Texas finished in second place with an 84-76 record, and only five games out of first place. Once again, there was hope for the future.

Martin and his Rangers did not do well the following season. Texas fell below .500 and Martin fell out of favor. Halfway through the season, Frank Lucchesi took over as manager. The team finished third in 1975 and tied for fourth in 1976.

Despite these losing years, Hargrove, Burroughs, and Harrah played well. The pitching improved with the addition of Gaylord Perry, Nelson Briles, and Bert Blyleven. The stage was set for 1977— the best season in Ranger history.

Rangers' first baseman Mike Hargrove during batting practice at Arlington Stadium. Hargrove won the AL Rookie of the Year Award in 1974.

# Ups And Downs

The 1977 season did not start out well. With the team at 31-31, new owner Brad Corbett fired Lucchesi after 62 games. Eddie Stankey and Connie Ryan filled in as managers. Finally, Billy Hunter took over. The Rangers won 60 games and lost 33 over the last two thirds of the season. But they did not win the division.

New players appeared in Ranger uniforms in 1978. Pitcher Jon Matlack came in a winter trade. Ferguson Jenkins returned after two seasons with the Boston Red Sox. Bert Blyleven was traded to Pittsburgh for outfielder Al Oliver. White Sox outfielder Bobby Bonds joined the team early in the season.

Though they seemed to be improved, the 1978 Rangers finished third with an 87-75 record. Oliver finished second in the AL batting race at .324. Bonds smacked a team-leading 29 homers. Designated hitter Richie Zisk led the team in RBIs with 85. Before the 1978 season ended, Hunter was fired. Pat Corrales replaced him for the coming season.

With Bump Wills at second base and Buddy Bell at third, the 1979 Rangers looked even better. Bell drove in 101 runs and hit 18 homers. Wills batted .273. Al Oliver hit .323. He was joined in the outfield by Mickey Rivers, who batted .300. The team finished third, five games back. The next year, however, the Rangers fell below .500 and finished in fourth place.

Rangers' pitcher Bert Blyleven is the picture of concentration as he kicks and readies for a pitch in a 1976 game against the New York Yankees.

Don Zimmer became manager in 1981, the year of the strike-shortened season. The Rangers finished second in the first half, third in the second half, and did not make the playoffs. But the team finally showed improvement. They played at a .543 pace, as Al Oliver again led the club in hitting with a .309 average. Pitcher Doc Medich, a Ranger since 1978, enjoyed his fourth straight winning season with a 10-6 record and a 3.08 ERA. Newly acquired left-hander Rick Honeycutt went 11-6 with a 3.30 ERA.

The 1982 Rangers started slow and never improved. By late July, Zimmer was gone. New manager Darrell Johnson saw the team finish with a 64-98 record, good for sixth place.

The bright spots were outfielder Larry Parrish and first baseman Dave Hostetler. Parrish would eventually become the Rangers' career home run leader with 156.

Third baseman Buddy Bell leaps for a ball in a 1985 game at Anaheim Stadium.

Mike Hargrove won the AL Rookie of the Year Award in 1974.

As a Washington Senator, Frank Howard led the team in home runs seven seasons in a row, leading the league in 1968 and 1970.

In 1979, third baseman Buddy Bell drove in 101 runs and hit 18 homers.

In his 1986 rookie season, outfielder Ruben Sierra hit 13 doubles, 10 triples, and 16 homers.

# Rangers

Hall-of-Fame pitcher Nolan Ryan started for the Rangers in 1989.

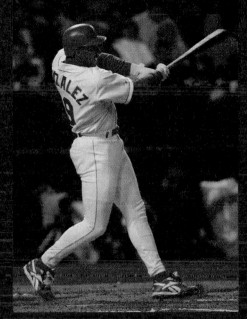

In 1993, Juan Gonzalez hit 46 homers for his second straight home run crown.

During the 1995 season, Mickey Tettleton hit a team-high 32 home runs.

Will Clark knocked in 92 runs during the 1995 season.

# More Managers

Over the next three seasons, Doug Rader took over as manager. In 1983, the Rangers got off to a fast start with a good team. Charlie Hough, Rick Honeycutt, Frank Tanana, Mike Smithson, and Danny Darwin formed a tough pitching staff. But without solid hitting, the Rangers did not finish with a winning record. No Ranger player appeared among the league leaders in any major categories. Even more frustrating, they seemed better than a last-place team, which they were in 1984 and 1985.

First baseman Pete O'Brien and outfielder Gary Ward showed promise. But the team could not make a run for the title. Rader left 22 games into the 1985 season. Bobby Valentine took over and coached the Rangers to a 62-99 season.

The 1986 Texas Rangers were not expected to do much because of their lack of experience. Rookie pitcher Bobby Witt surprised the league with an 11-9 record. Outfielder Pete Incaviglia came straight from Oklahoma State University and blasted 30 homers, tying the all-time team high. He also drove in 88 runs. Unfortunately, he also set an AL record with 185 strikeouts.

*Facing page:* Bobby Witt pitches during a July 8, 1989, game against the Oakland Athletics. The Rangers won 6-3.

Reliever Mitch Williams set a major-league record with 80 appearances. In just 113 games, rookie outfielder Ruben Sierra smacked 13 doubles, 10 triples, and 16 homers. Shortstop Scott Fletcher, acquired from the White Sox, batted .300.

From late May to late June, the Rangers led their division. But in the end they wilted in the hot Texas sun and settled for second place, five games behind the California Angels.

Right fielder Ruben Sierra goes up against the outfield wall in an attempt to catch a ball during a 1987 game against the Seattle Mariners.

Forty-four-year-old Nolan Ryan making his 25th start of the 1991 season for the Texas Rangers.

# Rebuilding

Instead of improving, the Texas Rangers got worse. In 1987 and 1988, the Rangers tumbled into sixth place. In 1989, the arrival of Hall-of-Fame pitcher Nolan Ryan, second baseman Julio Franco, and first baseman Rafael Palmeiro boosted the Rangers to fourth place. Then they finished third in 1990 and 1991.

In 1991, Franco became the first Ranger to win the AL batting crown, hitting .341. Palmeiro (.322) and Sierra (.307) were close behind. In 1992, after three straight .500-plus seasons, the Rangers fell to .475 and finished fourth. The pitching performed better than the hitting, as Kevin Brown posted a 22-11 mark and Jose Guzman a 16-11 record.

On August 31, Sierra, Witt, and Jeff Russell went to Oakland for slugger Jose Canseco. Kevin Kennedy replaced Toby Harrah, who earlier in the 1992 season replaced Valentine.

Before the 1993 season, Ryan announced that he would retire at the end of the year. With a powerful lineup behind him, the major league's all-time strikeout leader hoped to go out on a pennant-winning team. But instead, he suffered through an injury-plagued season, going 5-5 with 46 strikeouts in 66.1 innings.

Second baseman Julio Franco jumps to avoid a runner.

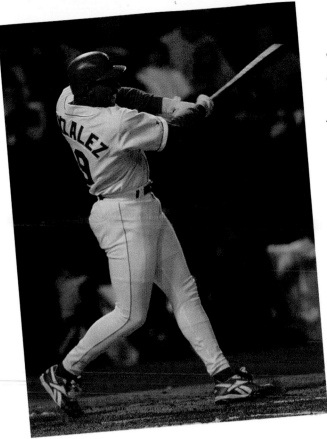

Juan Gonzalez takes a swing during a 1996 game against the Boston Red Sox.

In 1993, Kennedy guided the Rangers to a second-place finish in the AL West with an 86-76 record. Juan Gonzalez became a superstar, smacking 46 homers for his second consecutive home run title. He also led the team in hitting with a .310 batting average. Rafael Palmeiro proved to be one of the league's best power hitters. He banged out 37 homers and knocked in 105 runs. Dean Palmer surprised everyone with 33 home runs and 96 RBIs. David Hulse (.290), Julio Franco (.289), and Ivan Rodriguez (.273) showed much promise.

Closer Tom Henke had a career high in saves with 40. Starters Kenny Rogers (16-10), Kevin Brown (15-12), and Roger Pavlik (12-6) kept the Rangers in title contention for most of the season.

Jose Canseco was expected to contribute to the team's pennant drive. But he injured his elbow while pitching during a 15-1 blowout loss to the Boston Red Sox. Like Ryan, he sat out much of the year.

Will Clark tosses a ball to teammate Roger Pavlik for an out during a 1995 game against the California Angles.

# More Changes

Big changes occurred in 1994, hurting the Rangers' pennant hopes. Palmeiro, Franco, and Canseco left the team for more money. Though Texas ended the season with a 52-62 record, they finished first in the division. However, as luck would have it, the Rangers did not make post-season play. No team did. A players' strike washed away all World Series dreams in 1994.

In 1995, the Rangers had one of their better years. They posted a 41-31 home record and challenged for the division title the entire season. But like seasons before, they wilted in the hot Texas sun and fell short of first place by four games. Still, their 74-70 overall record was encouraging, and fans looked forward to improvement in 1996.

Star players like Mickey Tettleton gave them hope. He hit a team-high 32 home runs. Veteran Will Clark knocked in 92 runs, picking up the slack for injury-plagued Juan Gonzalez, who still managed to hit 27 homers and drive in 82 runs in only 90 games. Dean Palmer had another strong year as he batted .336 in 36 games before an injury ended his season. Fleet-footed Otis Nixon stole 50 bases, second best in the American League. And catcher Ivan Rodriguez, always solid defensively behind the plate, stepped up with his best offensive performance. He batted .303—second-best on the team—while driving in 67 runs.

The Rangers' pitching was disappointing. Starter Kenny Rogers posted an impressive 17-7 record with a 3.38 ERA, while reliever Jeff Russell notched 20 saves. But Roger Pavlik fell to 10-10 with a 4.37 ERA. Bobby Witt was injured most of the year, and Kevin Gross posted a 9-15 record. Overall, the Rangers' pitching staff finished with a 4.67 ERA, eighth-best in the American League.

Mickey Tettleton watches his three-run home run in a 1995 game against Seattle.

# A Pennant- Winning Season

In 1996, the Rangers captured their first division title. With Gonzalez and Palmer in the lineup for the whole season, the Rangers exploded offensively. The defense improved drastically, and shortstop Benji Gil was a large part of the reason. Pitchers Ken Hill and Mike Henneman filled the void left by the departure of Kenny Rogers and Jeff Russell.

After capturing the 1996 American League Western Division Pennant the Rangers had little time to celebrate. In the first round of the American League playoffs, the Rangers met the Eastern Champion New York Yankees.

Although the Rangers played better ball, it was the Yankees who came up the winner. Up 4-0 in the fourth inning of Game 4, the Rangers blew the lead for the third time in the series. Texas lost 6-4 and were eliminated from the playoffs three games to one.

The Rangers are improving every year. If the team fills a few more pieces in the puzzle, it won't be long before they have their first World Series Championship.

# Glossary

**All-Star:** A player who is voted by fans as the best player at one position in a given year.

**American League (AL):** An association of baseball teams formed in 1900 which make up one-half of the major leagues.

**American League Championship Series (ALCS):** A best-of-seven-game playoff with the winner going to the World Series to face the National League Champions.

**Batting Average:** A baseball statistic calculated by dividing a batter's hits by the number of times at bat.

**Earned Run Average (ERA):** A baseball statistic which calculates the average number of runs a pitcher gives up per nine innings of work.

**Fielding Average:** A baseball statistic which calculates a fielder's success rate based on the number of chances the player has to record an out.

**Hall of Fame:** A memorial for the greatest baseball players of all time located in Cooperstown, New York.

**Home Run (HR):** A play in baseball where a batter hits the ball over the outfield fence scoring everyone on base as well as the batter.

**Major Leagues:** The highest ranking associations of professional baseball teams in the world, currently consisting of the American and National Baseball Leagues.

**Minor Leagues:** A system of professional baseball leagues at levels below Major League Baseball.

**National League (NL):** An association of baseball teams formed in 1876 which make up one-half of the major leagues.

**National League Championship Series (NLCS):** A best-of-seven-game playoff with the winner going to the World Series to face the American League Champions.

**Pennant:** A flag which symbolizes the championship of a professional baseball league.

**Pitcher:** The player on a baseball team who throws the ball for the batter to hit. The pitcher stands on a mound and pitches the ball toward the strike zone area above the plate.

**Plate:** The place on a baseball field where a player stands to bat. It is used to determine the width of the strike zone. Forming the point of the diamond-shaped field, it is the final goal a base runner must reach to score a run.

**RBI:** A baseball statistic standing for *runs batted in*. Players receive an RBI for each run that scores on their hits.

**Rookie:** A first-year player, especially in a professional sport.

**Slugging Percentage:** A statistic which points out a player's ability to hit for extra bases by taking the number of total bases hit and dividing it by the number of at bats.

**Stolen Base:** A play in baseball when a base runner advances to the next base while the pitcher is delivering his pitch.

**Strikeout:** A play in baseball when a batter is called out for failing to put the ball in play after the pitcher has delivered three strikes.

**Triple Crown:** A rare accomplishment when a single player finishes a season leading their league in batting average, home runs, and RBIs. A pitcher can win a Triple Crown by leading the league in wins, ERA, and strikeouts.

**Walk:** A play in baseball when a batter receives four pitches out of the strike zone and is allowed to go to first base.

**World Series:** The championship of Major League Baseball played since 1903 between the pennant winners from the American and National Leagues.

# Index

## L

Lemon, Jim  4, 8
Long, Dale  7
Los Angeles Dodgers  8
Lucchesi, Frank  14, 15

## M

Mahoney, Jim  7
Martin, Billy  13, 14
Matlack, Jon  15
McMullen, Ken  8
Medich, Doc  17
Mincher, Don  11
Most Valuable Player Award 13

## N

New York Yankees  8
Nixon, Otis  27

## O

Oakland Athletics  11, 12, 24
O'Brien, Pat  20
Ohio State  8
Oliver, Al  15, 17
Osteen, Claude  7

## P

Palmeiro, Rafael  23, 25, 26
Palmer, Dean  4, 25, 27, 28
Parrish, Larry  17
Pavlik, Roger  25, 27
Perry, Gaylord  14
Piersall, Jimmy  7
Pittsburgh Pirates  15

## R

Rader, Doug  20
Randle, Lenny  13
Rivers, Mickey  15
Rodriguez, Ivan  25, 27
Rogers, Kenny  25, 27, 28
Rookie of the Year Award  8, 13
Russell, Jeff  24, 27, 28
Ryan, Connie  15
Ryan, Nolan  4, 23, 24, 25

## S

Short, Bob  12
Sierra, Ruben  22, 23, 24
Smithson, Mike  20
Spencer, Jim  12
Stankey, Eddie  15

## T

Tanana, Frank  20
Tasby, Willie  7
Tettleton, Mickey  26
Tovar, Cesar  13

## V

Valentine, Bobby  4, 20, 24
Vernon, Mickey  4, 7

## W

Ward, Gary  20
Washington Senators  4, 6, 7, 8, 11, 12
Williams, Mitch  22
Williams, Ted  4, 8, 11, 12
Wills, Bump  15
Witt, Bobby  20, 24, 27
Woodling, Gene  7
World Series  8, 26

## Z

Zimmer, Don  4, 17
Zisk, Richie  15